MW01136204

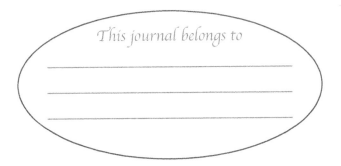

This journal belongs to

_____

_____

_____

Grateful FAITH

A Gratitude Journal

Grateful FAITH

A 180-day gratitude journal to help you trust
God today by giving thanks to Him each day.

Bonnie Edson

This journal is dedicated to all those who long
to give thanks to God and to trust Him.

Introduction
Grateful FAITH

"Lord, I believe, help my unbelief!" Mark 9:24.
That verse has been my go-to so many times that how many doesn't matter anymore. I was trying to be grateful to God and also struggling to trust Him. So I began, "What questions should I be asking you God that will make me see what I have from you and trust in you each day going forward?" Each day as I sat asking this one question of God, He gave me questions in response. This journal are the questions He gave me.

How to use
Grateful FAITH

Grateful Faith is set up for you to use it in the morning and evening. The first four prompts are to be done in the morning before you get going on your day. These focus you on God and gratefulness and trust. The last one, which is shaded, is for reflection on God before you go to bed. This design helps you notice what you're grateful for to set you up for your day but also remind you of God's presence as you end your day.

If you're like me and want a little more information, here are some ideas:
"I am grateful for" Be grateful first. *"Enter His gates with thanksgiving and His courts with praise. Give thanks to Him and praise His name." Psalm 100:4.* This can be anything you're grateful for today. It may be your family, your dog, spouse, or even the weather. It can be big and major like another day for you or someone you love or something simple like the feel of a breeze.

"Thank you LORD that You are Good, Faithful and Sovereign, I will trust You in this way today." This section gets you thinking a little more. What do you want or need to trust God for today? It may be the same thing you wrote yesterday and the day before or it could be something completely different. After doing this for a little while you will grow in what you want to trust Him with. Let Him speak to you and relax and speak to Him. Ask...

"You, God, say that I am" It is so important that we hear and learn and know who God says we are. Faith in God is believing God. Believe what He says about you. Think about if it's different than what you say. Believe Him.

"Dear God" is simply your prayer. What do you want to say to Him, confess to Him, ask of Him? This is your journal, your thoughts, your conversation with God.

"How did I see God's goodness, faithfulness and sovereignty today?" Look back over your day, how did you see God? Perhaps in a sunset, a word from someone, a smile. Or did He show up in a stop sign, a conviction about something, protecting you from something? If you're not sure, ask Him where He is.

Date _____ / _____ / 20_____

In the beginning God created the heavens and the earth.

Genesis 1:1

I am grateful for...

....

....

....

Thank You LORD that You are Good, Faithful and Sovereign,
I will trust You in this way today...

....

....

....

You, God, say that I am...

....

....

Dear God...

....

....

....

....

....

....

....

....

....

....

....

....

....

....

How did I see God's goodness, faithfulness and sovereignty today?

....

....

Date _____ / _____ / 20_____

I will never leave you or abandon you.

Hebrews 13:5

I am grateful for...

....
....
....

Thank You LORD that You are Good, Faithful and Sovereign,
I will trust You in this way today...

....
....
....

You, God, say that I am...

....
....

Dear God...

....
....
....
....
....
....
....
....
....
....
....
....
....
....

How did I see God's goodness, faithfulness and sovereignty today?

....
....

Date _____ / _____ / 20_____

But anyone joined to the Lord is one spirit with him.

1 Corinthians 6:17

I am grateful for...

....

....

....

Thank You LORD that You are Good, Faithful and Sovereign,
I will trust You in this way today...

....

....

....

You, God, say that I am...

....

....

Dear God...

....

....

....

....

....

....

....

....

....

....

....

....

....

....

How did I see God's goodness, faithfulness and sovereignty today?

....

....

Date _____ / _____ / 20_____

I will both lie down and sleep in peace, for you alone,
LORD, make me live in safety.

I am grateful for...

....

....

....

Thank You LORD that You are Good, Faithful and Sovereign,
I will trust You in this way today...

....

....

....

You, God, say that I am...

....

....

Dear God...

....

....

....

....

....

....

....

....

....

....

....

....

....

....

How did I see God's goodness, faithfulness and sovereignty today?

....

....

Date _____ / _____ / 20_____

Don't you know that your body is a temple of the Holy Spirit who is in you, whom you have from God? You are not your own, for you were bought at a price. So glorify God with your body.

I am grateful for...   *1 Corinthians 6:19-20*

....
....
....

Thank You LORD that You are Good, Faithful and Sovereign,
I will trust You in this way today...

....
....
....

You, God, say that I am...

....
....

Dear God...

....
....
....
....
....
....
....
....
....
....
....
....
....

How did I see God's goodness, faithfulness and sovereignty today?

....
....

Date _____ / _____ / 20_____

Let us hold on to the confession of our hope without wavering,
since he who promised is faithful.

Hebrews 10:23

I am grateful for...

....

....

....

Thank You LORD that You are Good, Faithful and Sovereign,
I will trust You in this way today...

....

....

....

You, God, say that I am...

....

....

Dear God...

....

....

....

....

....

....

....

....

....

....

....

....

....

How did I see God's goodness, faithfulness and sovereignty today?

....

....

Date _____ / _____ / 20_____

Rest in God alone, my soul, for my hope comes from him.

Psalm 62:5

I am grateful for...

....

....

....

Thank You LORD that You are Good, Faithful and Sovereign,
I will trust You in this way today...

....

....

....

You, God, say that I am...

....

....

Dear God...

....

....

....

....

....

....

....

....

....

....

....

....

....

....

....

How did I see God's goodness, faithfulness and sovereignty today?

....

....

Date _____ / _____ / 20_____

For if, while we were enemies, we were reconciled to God through the death of his Son, then how much more, having been reconciled, will we be saved by his life.

I am grateful for...   *Romans 5:10*

....

....

....

Thank You LORD that You are Good, Faithful and Sovereign,
I will trust You in this way today...

....

....

....

You, God, say that I am...

....

....

Dear God...

....

....

....

....

....

....

....

....

....

....

....

....

....

....

How did I see God's goodness, faithfulness and sovereignty today?

....

....

Date _____ / _____ / 20_____

But to all who did receive him, he gave them the right to be children of God, to those who believe in his name.

I am grateful for...

....

....

....

Thank You LORD that You are Good, Faithful and Sovereign,
I will trust You in this way today...

....

....

....

You, God, say that I am...

....

....

Dear God...

....

....

....

....

....

....

....

....

....

....

....

....

....

....

How did I see God's goodness, faithfulness and sovereignty today?

....

....

Date _____ / _____ / 20_____

"But you," he asked them, *"who do you say that I am?"* Simon Peter
answered, *"You are the Messiah the Son of the living God."*

Matthew 16:15-16

I am grateful for...

....
....
....

Thank You LORD that You are Good, Faithful and Sovereign,
I will trust You in this way today...

....
....
....

You, God, say that I am...

....
....

Dear God...

....
....
....
....
....
....
....
....
....
....
....
....
....
....

How did I see God's goodness, faithfulness and sovereignty today?

....
....

Date _____ / _____ / 20_____

The LORD will fulfill his purpose for me. LORD, your faithful love endures forever; do not abandon the work of your hands.

Psalm 138:8

I am grateful for...

....

....

....

Thank You LORD that You are Good, Faithful and Sovereign,
I will trust You in this way today...

....

....

....

You, God, say that I am...

....

....

Dear God...

....

....

....

....

....

....

....

....

....

....

....

....

....

....

How did I see God's goodness, faithfulness and sovereignty today?

....

....

Date _____ / _____ / 20_____

For God has not given us a spirit of fear, but one of power, love, and sound judgment.

I am grateful for...

....

....

....

Thank You LORD that You are Good, Faithful and Sovereign,
I will trust You in this way today...

....

....

....

You, God, say that I am...

....

....

Dear God...

....

....

....

....

....

....

....

....

....

....

....

....

....

How did I see God's goodness, faithfulness and sovereignty today?

....

....

Date _____ / _____ / 20_____

But you will receive power when the Holy Spirit has come on you, and you will be my witnesses in Jerusalem, in all Judea and Samaria, and to the end of the earth.

I am grateful for...   *Acts 1:8*

....

....

....

Thank You LORD that You are Good, Faithful and Sovereign,
I will trust You in this way today...

....

....

....

You, God, say that I am...

....

....

Dear God...

....

....

....

....

....

....

....

....

....

....

....

....

....

....

How did I see God's goodness, faithfulness and sovereignty today?

....

....

Date _____ / _____ / 20_____

*He has rescued us from the domain of darkness and transferred us
into the kingdom of the Son he loves.*

Colossians 1:13

I am grateful for...

....
....
....

Thank You LORD that You are Good, Faithful and Sovereign,
I will trust You in this way today...

....
....
....

You, God, say that I am...

....
....

Dear God...

....
....
....
....
....
....
....
....
....
....
....
....
....
....

How did I see God's goodness, faithfulness and sovereignty today?

....
....

Date _____ / _____ / 20_____

LORD, your word is forever; it is firmly fixed in heaven.

Psalm 119:89

I am grateful for...

....

....

....

Thank You LORD that You are Good, Faithful and Sovereign,
I will trust You in this way today...

....

....

....

You, God, say that I am...

....

....

Dear God...

....

....

....

....

....

....

....

....

....

....

....

....

....

....

How did I see God's goodness, faithfulness and sovereignty today?

....

....

Date _____ / _____ / 20_____

In him we have boldness and confident access through faith in him.

I am grateful for...

....

....

....

Thank You LORD that You are Good, Faithful and Sovereign,
I will trust You in this way today...

....

....

....

You, God, say that I am...

....

....

Dear God...

....

....

....

....

....

....

....

....

....

....

....

....

....

....

How did I see God's goodness, faithfulness and sovereignty today?

....

....

Date _____ / _____ / 20_____

I do not call you servants anymore, because a servant doesn't know what his master is doing. I have called you friends, because I have made known to you everything I have heard from my Father.

I am grateful for...   John 15:15

....

....

....

Thank You LORD that You are Good, Faithful and Sovereign,
I will trust You in this way today...

....

....

....

You, God, say that I am...

....

....

Dear God...

....

....

....

....

....

....

....

....

....

....

....

....

....

....

How did I see God's goodness, faithfulness and sovereignty today?

....

....

Date _____ / _____ / 20_____

I will sing to the LORD all my life;
I will sing praise to my God while I live.

Psalm 104:33

I am grateful for...

....
....
....

Thank You LORD that You are Good, Faithful and Sovereign,
I will trust You in this way today...

....
....
....

You, God, say that I am...

....
....

Dear God...

....
....
....
....
....
....
....
....
....
....
....
....
....
....

How did I see God's goodness, faithfulness and sovereignty today?

....
....

Date _____ / _____ / 20_____

Blessed is the God and Father of our Lord Jesus Christ, who has blessed us with every spiritual blessing in the heavens in Christ.

Ephesians 1:3

I am grateful for...

....

....

....

Thank You LORD that You are Good, Faithful and Sovereign,
I will trust You in this way today...

....

....

....

You, God, say that I am...

....

....

Dear God...

....

....

....

....

....

....

....

....

....

....

....

....

....

....

How did I see God's goodness, faithfulness and sovereignty today?

....

....

Date _____ / _____ / 20_____

*You did not choose me, but I chose you. I appointed you to go
and produce fruit and that your fruit should remain,
so that whatever you ask the Father in my name, he will give you.*

I am grateful for...   *John 15:16*

....

....

....

Thank You LORD that You are Good, Faithful and Sovereign,
I will trust You in this way today...

....

....

....

You, God, say that I am...

....

....

Dear God...

....

....

....

....

....

....

....

....

....

....

....

....

....

....

How did I see God's goodness, faithfulness and sovereignty today?

....

....

Date _____ / _____ / 20_____

And not only that, but we also rejoice in God through our Lord Jesus Christ, through whom we have now received this reconciliation.

I am grateful for...

....

....

....

Thank You LORD that You are Good, Faithful and Sovereign,
I will trust You in this way today...

....

....

....

You, God, say that I am...

....

....

Dear God...

....

....

....

....

....

....

....

....

....

....

....

....

....

....

How did I see God's goodness, faithfulness and sovereignty today?

....

....

Date _____ / _____ / 20_____

The one who lives under the protection of the Most High dwells in the shadow of the Almighty. I will say concerning the LORD, who is my refuge and my fortress, my God in whom I trust:

I am grateful for...   *Psalm 91:1-2*

....

....

....

Thank You LORD that You are Good, Faithful and Sovereign,
I will trust You in this way today...

....

....

....

You, God, say that I am...

....

....

Dear God...

....

....

....

....

....

....

....

....

....

....

....

....

....

....

How did I see God's goodness, faithfulness and sovereignty today?

....

....

Date _____ / _____ / 20_____

For we are his workmanship, created in Christ Jesus for good works,
which God prepared ahead of time for us to do.

Ephesians 2:10

I am grateful for...

....

....

....

Thank You LORD that You are Good, Faithful and Sovereign,
I will trust You in this way today...

....

....

....

You, God, say that I am...

....

....

Dear God...

....

....

....

....

....

....

....

....

....

....

....

....

....

....

How did I see God's goodness, faithfulness and sovereignty today?

....

....

Date _____ / _____ / 20_____

Now you are the body of Christ, and individual members of it.

1 Corinthians 12:27

I am grateful for...

....
....
....

Thank You LORD that You are Good, Faithful and Sovereign,
I will trust You in this way today...

....
....
....

You, God, say that I am...

....
....

Dear God...

....
....
....
....
....
....
....
....
....
....
....
....
....

How did I see God's goodness, faithfulness and sovereignty today?

....
....

Date _____ / _____ / 20_____

So God created man in his own image; he created him in the image of God; he created them male and female.

Genesis 1:27

I am grateful for...

....

....

....

Thank You LORD that You are Good, Faithful and Sovereign,
I will trust You in this way today...

....

....

....

You, God, say that I am...

....

....

Dear God...

....

....

....

....

....

....

....

....

....

....

....

....

....

....

How did I see God's goodness, faithfulness and sovereignty today?

....

....

Date _____ / _____ / 20_____

By faith Abraham, when he was called, obeyed and set out for a place
that he was going to receive as an inheritance. He went out,
even though he did not know where he was going.

I am grateful for...   *Hebrews 11:8*

....

....

....

Thank You LORD that You are Good, Faithful and Sovereign,
I will trust You in this way today...

....

....

....

You, God, say that I am...

....

....

Dear God...

....

....

....

....

....

....

....

....

....

....

....

....

....

....

....

How did I see God's goodness, faithfulness and sovereignty today?

....

....

Date _____ / _____ / 20_____

I delight to do your will, my God,
and your instruction is deep within me.

Psalm 40:8

I am grateful for...

....

....

....

Thank You LORD that You are Good, Faithful and Sovereign,
I will trust You in this way today...

....

....

....

You, God, say that I am...

....

....

Dear God...

....

....

....

....

....

....

....

....

....

....

....

....

....

How did I see God's goodness, faithfulness and sovereignty today?

....

....

Date _____ / _____ / 20_____

For the one who sanctifies and those who are sanctified
all have one Father. That is why Jesus is not ashamed to call them
brothers and sisters.

I am grateful for...   *Hebrews 2:11*

....

....

....

Thank You LORD that You are Good, Faithful and Sovereign,
I will trust You in this way today...

....

....

....

You, God, say that I am...

....

....

Dear God...

....

....

....

....

....

....

....

....

....

....

....

....

....

....

How did I see God's goodness, faithfulness and sovereignty today?

....

....

Date _____ / _____ / 20_____

For God loved the world in this way: He gave his one and only Son, so that everyone who believes in him will not perish but have eternal life.

John 3:16

I am grateful for...

....

....

....

Thank You LORD that You are Good, Faithful and Sovereign,
I will trust You in this way today...

....

....

....

You, God, say that I am...

....

....

Dear God...

....

....

....

....

....

....

....

....

....

....

....

....

....

....

How did I see God's goodness, faithfulness and sovereignty today?

....

....

Date _____ / _____ / 20_____

Let them give thanks to the LORD for his faithful love
and his wondrous works for all humanity.

Psalm 107:21

I am grateful for...

....

....

....

Thank You LORD that You are Good, Faithful and Sovereign,
I will trust You in this way today...

....

....

....

You, God, say that I am...

....

....

Dear God...

....

....

....

....

....

....

....

....

....

....

....

....

....

How did I see God's goodness, faithfulness and sovereignty today?

....

....

Date _____ / _____ / 20_____

For we walk by faith, not by sight.

2 Corinthians 5:7

I am grateful for...

....

....

....

Thank You LORD that You are Good, Faithful and Sovereign,
I will trust You in this way today...

....

....

....

You, God, say that I am...

....

....

Dear God...

....

....

....

....

....

....

....

....

....

....

....

....

....

How did I see God's goodness, faithfulness and sovereignty today?

....

....

Date _____ / _____ / 20_____

Now if any of you lacks wisdom, he should ask God -- who gives to all generously and ungrudgingly -- and it will be given to him.

James 1:5

I am grateful for...

....
....
....

Thank You LORD that You are Good, Faithful and Sovereign,
I will trust You in this way today...

....
....
....

You, God, say that I am...

....
....

Dear God...

....
....
....
....
....
....
....
....
....
....
....
....
....
....

How did I see God's goodness, faithfulness and sovereignty today?

....
....

Date _____ / _____ / 20_____

But now he has reconciled you by his physical body through his death,
to present you holy, faultless, and blameless before him.

Colossians 1:22

I am grateful for...

....

....

....

Thank You LORD that You are Good, Faithful and Sovereign,
I will trust You in this way today...

....

....

....

You, God, say that I am...

....

....

Dear God...

....

....

....

....

....

....

....

....

....

....

....

....

....

How did I see God's goodness, faithfulness and sovereignty today?

....

....

Date _____ / _____ / 20_____

Commit your way to the LORD; trust in him, and he will act.

Psalm 37:5

I am grateful for...

....

....

....

Thank You LORD that You are Good, Faithful and Sovereign,
I will trust You in this way today...

....

....

....

You, God, say that I am...

....

....

Dear God...

....

....

....

....

....

....

....

....

....

....

....

....

....

How did I see God's goodness, faithfulness and sovereignty today?

....

....

Date _____ / _____ / 20_____

Oh, Lord GOD! You yourself made the heavens
and earth by your great power and with your outstretched arm.
Nothing is too difficult for you!

Jeremiah 32:17

I am grateful for...

....

....

....

Thank You LORD that You are Good, Faithful and Sovereign,
I will trust You in this way today...

....

....

....

You, God, say that I am...

....

....

Dear God...

....

....

....

....

....

....

....

....

....

....

....

....

....

How did I see God's goodness, faithfulness and sovereignty today?

....

....

Date _____ / _____ / 20_____

Haven't I commanded you: be strong and courageous? Do not be afraid or discouraged, for the LORD your God is with you wherever you go.

Joshua 1:9

I am grateful for...

....
....
....

Thank You LORD that You are Good, Faithful and Sovereign,
I will trust You in this way today...

....
....
....

You, God, say that I am...

....
....

Dear God...

....
....
....
....
....
....
....
....
....
....
....
....
....
....

How did I see God's goodness, faithfulness and sovereignty today?

....
....

Date _____ / _____ / 20_____

He sent his word and healed them; he rescued them from the Pit.

I am grateful for...

....

....

....

Thank You LORD that You are Good, Faithful and Sovereign,
I will trust You in this way today...

....

....

....

You, God, say that I am...

....

....

Dear God...

....

....

....

....

....

....

....

....

....

....

....

....

....

How did I see God's goodness, faithfulness and sovereignty today?

....

....

Date _____ / _____ / 20_____

How much more then, since we have now been declared righteous by his blood, will we be saved through him from wrath.

Romans 5:9

I am grateful for...

....

....

....

Thank You LORD that You are Good, Faithful and Sovereign,
I will trust You in this way today...

....

....

....

You, God, say that I am...

....

....

Dear God...

....

....

....

....

....

....

....

....

....

....

....

....

....

....

How did I see God's goodness, faithfulness and sovereignty today?

....

....

Date _____ / _____ / 20_____

Jesus said to him, "If you can? Everything is possible for the one who believes." Immediately the father of the boy cried out, "I do believe; help my unbelief!"

Mark 9:23-24

I am grateful for...

....

....

....

Thank You LORD that You are Good, Faithful and Sovereign,
I will trust You in this way today...

....

....

....

You, God, say that I am...

....

....

Dear God...

....

....

....

....

....

....

....

....

....

....

....

....

....

How did I see God's goodness, faithfulness and sovereignty today?

....

....

Date _____ / _____ / 20_____

Take up my yoke and learn from me, because I am lowly and humble in heart, and you will find rest for your souls.

Matthew 11:29

I am grateful for...

....

....

....

Thank You LORD that You are Good, Faithful and Sovereign,
I will trust You in this way today...

....

....

....

You, God, say that I am...

....

....

Dear God...

....

....

....

....

....

....

....

....

....

....

....

....

....

....

How did I see God's goodness, faithfulness and sovereignty today?

....

....

Date _____ / _____ / 20_____

You are the light of the world.
A city situated on a hill cannot be hidden.

I am grateful for...

....

....

....

Thank You LORD that You are Good, Faithful and Sovereign,
I will trust You in this way today...

....

....

....

You, God, say that I am...

....

....

Dear God...

....

....

....

....

....

....

....

....

....

....

....

....

....

....

How did I see God's goodness, faithfulness and sovereignty today?

....

....

Date _____ / _____ / 20_____

Satisfy us in the morning with your faithful love so that we may shout with joy and be glad all our days.

Psalm 90:14

I am grateful for...

....
....
....

Thank You LORD that You are Good, Faithful and Sovereign,
I will trust You in this way today...

....
....
....

You, God, say that I am...

....
....

Dear God...

....
....
....
....
....
....
....
....
....
....
....
....
....
....

How did I see God's goodness, faithfulness and sovereignty today?

....
....

Date _____ / _____ / 20_____

But our citizenship is in heaven, and we eagerly wait for a Savior from there, the Lord Jesus Christ.

Philippians 3:20

I am grateful for...

....

....

....

Thank You LORD that You are Good, Faithful and Sovereign,
I will trust You in this way today...

....

....

....

You, God, say that I am...

....

....

Dear God...

....

....

....

....

....

....

....

....

....

....

....

....

....

How did I see God's goodness, faithfulness and sovereignty today?

....

....

Date _____ / _____ / 20_____

He was with God in the beginning.

John 1:2

I am grateful for...

....

....

....

Thank You LORD that You are Good, Faithful and Sovereign,
I will trust You in this way today...

....

....

....

You, God, say that I am...

....

....

Dear God...

....

....

....

....

....

....

....

....

....

....

....

....

....

....

How did I see God's goodness, faithfulness and sovereignty today?

....

....

Date _____ / _____ / 20_____

He made the one who did not know sin to be sin for us, so that in him we might become the righteousness of God.

2 Corinthians 5:21

I am grateful for...

....

....

....

Thank You LORD that You are Good, Faithful and Sovereign,
I will trust You in this way today...

....

....

....

You, God, say that I am...

....

....

Dear God...

....

....

....

....

....

....

....

....

....

....

....

....

....

How did I see God's goodness, faithfulness and sovereignty today?

....

....

Date _____ / _____ / 20_____

I called to the LORD in distress;
the LORD answered me and put me in a spacious place.

I am grateful for...

....

....

....

Thank You LORD that You are Good, Faithful and Sovereign,
I will trust You in this way today...

....

....

....

You, God, say that I am...

....

....

Dear God...

....

....

....

....

....

....

....

....

....

....

....

....

....

....

How did I see God's goodness, faithfulness and sovereignty today?

....

....

Date _____ / _____ / 20_____

If we confess our sins, he is faithful and righteous to forgive us our sins and to cleanse us from all unrighteousness.

1 John 1:9

I am grateful for...

....

....

....

Thank You LORD that You are Good, Faithful and Sovereign,
I will trust You in this way today...

....

....

....

You, God, say that I am...

....

....

Dear God...

....

....

....

....

....

....

....

....

....

....

....

....

....

How did I see God's goodness, faithfulness and sovereignty today?

....

....

Date _____ / _____ / 20_____

But your love has delivered me from the Pit of destruction,
for you have thrown all my sins behind your back.

Isaiah 38:17b

I am grateful for...

....
....
....

Thank You LORD that You are Good, Faithful and Sovereign,
I will trust You in this way today...

....
....
....

You, God, say that I am...

....
....

Dear God...

....
....
....
....
....
....
....
....
....
....
....
....
....
....

How did I see God's goodness, faithfulness and sovereignty today?

....
....

Date _____ / _____ / 20_____

I am oppressed and needy; may the Lord think of me.
You are my helper and my deliverer; my God, do not delay.

I am grateful for...

....

....

....

Thank You LORD that You are Good, Faithful and Sovereign,
I will trust You in this way today...

....

....

....

You, God, say that I am...

....

....

Dear God...

....

....

....

....

....

....

....

....

....

....

....

....

....

....

How did I see God's goodness, faithfulness and sovereignty today?

....

....

Date _____ / _____ / 20_____

The LORD's blessing enriches, and he adds no painful effort to it.

Proverbs 10:22

I am grateful for...

....

....

....

Thank You LORD that You are Good, Faithful and Sovereign,
I will trust You in this way today...

....

....

....

You, God, say that I am...

....

....

Dear God...

....

....

....

....

....

....

....

....

....

....

....

....

....

How did I see God's goodness, faithfulness and sovereignty today?

....

....

Date _____ / _____ / 20_____

My flesh and my heart may fail, but God is the strength of my heart, my portion forever.

Psalm 73:26

I am grateful for...

....

....

....

Thank You LORD that You are Good, Faithful and Sovereign,
I will trust You in this way today...

....

....

....

You, God, say that I am...

....

....

Dear God...

....

....

....

....

....

....

....

....

....

....

....

....

....

....

How did I see God's goodness, faithfulness and sovereignty today?

....

....

Date _____ / _____ / 20_____

When Jesus heard it, he answered him,
"Don't be afraid. Only believe, and she will be saved."

Luke 8:50

I am grateful for...

....

....

....

Thank You LORD that You are Good, Faithful and Sovereign,
I will trust You in this way today...

....

....

....

You, God, say that I am...

....

....

Dear God...

....

....

....

....

....

....

....

....

....

....

....

....

....

....

How did I see God's goodness, faithfulness and sovereignty today?

....

....

Date _____ / _____ / 20_____

Indeed, we have all received grace upon grace from his fullness.

John 1:16

I am grateful for...

....
....
....

Thank You LORD that You are Good, Faithful and Sovereign,
I will trust You in this way today...

....
....
....

You, God, say that I am...

....
....

Dear God...

....
....
....
....
....
....
....
....
....
....
....
....
....
....

How did I see God's goodness, faithfulness and sovereignty today?

....
....

Date _____ / _____ / 20_____

For you died, and your life is hidden with Christ in God.

Colossians 3:3

I am grateful for...

....
....
....

Thank You LORD that You are Good, Faithful and Sovereign,
I will trust You in this way today...

....
....
....

You, God, say that I am...

....
....

Dear God...

....
....
....
....
....
....
....
....
....
....
....
....
....
....

How did I see God's goodness, faithfulness and sovereignty today?

....
....

Date _____ / _____ / 20_____

Let those who want my vindication shout for joy and be glad;
let them continually say,
"The LORD be exalted. He takes pleasure in his servant's well being."

Psalm 35:27

I am grateful for...

....

....

....

Thank You LORD that You are Good, Faithful and Sovereign,
I will trust You in this way today...

....

....

....

You, God, say that I am...

....

....

Dear God...

....

....

....

....

....

....

....

....

....

....

....

....

....

....

How did I see God's goodness, faithfulness and sovereignty today?

....

....

Date _____ / _____ / 20_____

Who can separate us from the love of Christ? Can affliction or distress or persecution or famine or nakedness or danger or sword?

Romans 8:35

I am grateful for...

....

....

....

Thank You LORD that You are Good, Faithful and Sovereign,
I will trust You in this way today...

....

....

....

You, God, say that I am...

....

....

Dear God...

....

....

....

....

....

....

....

....

....

....

....

....

....

How did I see God's goodness, faithfulness and sovereignty today?

....

....

Date _____ / _____ / 20_____

The Lord God took the man and placed him in the garden of Eden to work it and watch over it.

Genesis 2:15

I am grateful for...

....

....

....

Thank You LORD that You are Good, Faithful and Sovereign,
I will trust You in this way today...

....

....

....

You, God, say that I am...

....

....

Dear God...

....

....

....

....

....

....

....

....

....

....

....

....

....

....

How did I see God's goodness, faithfulness and sovereignty today?

....

....

Date _____ / _____ / 20_____

But I will hope continually and will praise you more and more.

I am grateful for...

....
....
....

Thank You LORD that You are Good, Faithful and Sovereign,
I will trust You in this way today...

....
....
....

You, God, say that I am...

....
....

Dear God...

....
....
....
....
....
....
....
....
....
....
....
....
....
....
....

How did I see God's goodness, faithfulness and sovereignty today?

....
....

Date _____ / _____ / 20_____

Do not fear, for I am with you; do not be afraid, for I am your God.
I will strengthen you; I will help you; I will hold on to you with my
righteous right hand.

Isaiah 41:10

I am grateful for...

....

....

....

Thank You LORD that You are Good, Faithful and Sovereign,
I will trust You in this way today...

....

....

....

You, God, say that I am...

....

....

Dear God...

....

....

....

....

....

....

....

....

....

....

....

....

....

....

How did I see God's goodness, faithfulness and sovereignty today?

....

....

Date _____ / _____ / 20_____

Be sober-minded, be alert. Your adversary the devil is prowling around like a roaring lion, looking for anyone he can devour.

1 Peter 5:8

I am grateful for...

....
....
....

Thank You LORD that You are Good, Faithful and Sovereign,
I will trust You in this way today...

....
....
....

You, God, say that I am...

....
....

Dear God...

....
....
....
....
....
....
....
....
....
....
....
....
....

How did I see God's goodness, faithfulness and sovereignty today?

....
....

Date _____ / _____ / 20_____

For the Gentiles eagerly seek all these things, and your heavenly Father knows that you need them. But seek first the kingdom of God and his righteousness, and all these things will be provided for you.
Matthew 6:32-33

I am grateful for...

....

....

....

Thank You LORD that You are Good, Faithful and Sovereign,
I will trust You in this way today...

....

....

....

You, God, say that I am...

....

....

Dear God...

....

....

....

....

....

....

....

....

....

....

....

....

....

....

How did I see God's goodness, faithfulness and sovereignty today?

....

....

Date _____ / _____ / 20_____

Open my eyes so that I may contemplate wondrous things from your instruction.

Psalm 119:18

I am grateful for...

....

....

....

Thank You LORD that You are Good, Faithful and Sovereign,
I will trust You in this way today...

....

....

....

You, God, say that I am...

....

....

Dear God...

....

....

....

....

....

....

....

....

....

....

....

....

....

....

How did I see God's goodness, faithfulness and sovereignty today?

....

....

Date _____ / _____ / 20_____

For this is what love for God is: to keep his commands.
And his commands are not a burden, because everyone who has
been born of God conquers the world. This is the victory that has
conquered the world: our faith.
I am grateful for...   *1 John 5:3-4*

....

....

....

Thank You LORD that You are Good, Faithful and Sovereign,
I will trust You in this way today...

....

....

....

You, God, say that I am...

....

....

Dear God...

....

....

....

....

....

....

....

....

....

....

....

....

How did I see God's goodness, faithfulness and sovereignty today?

....

....

Date _____ / _____ / 20_____

So I say to you, ask, and it will be given to you. Seek, and you will find. Knock, and the door will be opened to you.

I am grateful for...

....

....

....

Thank You LORD that You are Good, Faithful and Sovereign,
I will trust You in this way today...

....

....

....

You, God, say that I am...

....

....

Dear God...

....

....

....

....

....

....

....

....

....

....

....

....

....

....

How did I see God's goodness, faithfulness and sovereignty today?

....

....

Date _____ / _____ / 20_____

I called to the LORD, who is worthy of praise,
and I was saved from my enemies.

Psalm 18:3

I am grateful for...

....

....

....

Thank You LORD that You are Good, Faithful and Sovereign,
I will trust You in this way today...

....

....

....

You, God, say that I am...

....

....

Dear God...

....

....

....

....

....

....

....

....

....

....

....

....

....

How did I see God's goodness, faithfulness and sovereignty today?

....

....

Date _____ / _____ / 20_____

For God is not unjust; he will not forget your work
and the love you demonstrated for his name by serving the saints -
and by continuing to serve them.

I am grateful for...   *Hebrews 6:10*

....

....

....

Thank You LORD that You are Good, Faithful and Sovereign,
I will trust You in this way today...

....

....

....

You, God, say that I am...

....

....

Dear God...

....

....

....

....

....

....

....

....

....

....

....

....

....

How did I see God's goodness, faithfulness and sovereignty today?

....

....

Date _____ / _____ / 20_____

Whatever you do, do it from the heart, as something done for the Lord and not for people, knowing that you will receive the reward of an inheritance from the Lord. You serve the Lord Christ.

Colossians 3:23-24

I am grateful for...

....

....

....

Thank You LORD that You are Good, Faithful and Sovereign,
I will trust You in this way today...

....

....

....

You, God, say that I am...

....

....

Dear God...

....

....

....

....

....

....

....

....

....

....

....

....

....

....

....

How did I see God's goodness, faithfulness and sovereignty today?

....

....

Date _____ / _____ / 20_____

It is good to give thanks to the LORD, to sing praise to your name, Most High, to declare your faithful love in the morning and your faithfulness at night.

I am grateful for...

Psalm 92:1-2

....

....

....

Thank You LORD that You are Good, Faithful and Sovereign,
I will trust You in this way today...

....

....

....

You, God, say that I am...

....

....

Dear God...

....

....

....

....

....

....

....

....

....

....

....

....

....

How did I see God's goodness, faithfulness and sovereignty today?

....

....

What then are we to say about these things?
If God is for us, who is against us?

I am grateful for...

....

....

....

Thank You LORD that You are Good, Faithful and Sovereign,
I will trust You in this way today...

....

....

....

You, God, say that I am...

....

....

Dear God...

....

....

....

....

....

....

....

....

....

....

....

....

....

....

How did I see God's goodness, faithfulness and sovereignty today?

....

....

Date _____ / _____ / 20_____

Therefore, through him let us continually offer up to God a sacrifice of
praise, that is, the fruit of lips that confess his name.

Hebrews 13:15

I am grateful for...

....

....

....

Thank You LORD that You are Good, Faithful and Sovereign,
I will trust You in this way today...

....

....

....

You, God, say that I am...

....

....

Dear God...

....

....

....

....

....

....

....

....

....

....

....

....

....

....

How did I see God's goodness, faithfulness and sovereignty today?

....

....

Date _____ / _____ / 20_____

I will rejoice and be glad in your faithful love because you have seen my affliction. You know the troubles of my soul.

Psalm 31:7

I am grateful for...

....

....

....

Thank You LORD that You are Good, Faithful and Sovereign,
I will trust You in this way today...

....

....

....

You, God, say that I am...

....

....

Dear God...

....

....

....

....

....

....

....

....

....

....

....

....

....

How did I see God's goodness, faithfulness and sovereignty today?

....

....

Date _____ / _____ / 20_____

In the beginning was the Word, and the Word was with God,
and the Word was God.

John 1:1

I am grateful for...

....

....

....

Thank You LORD that You are Good, Faithful and Sovereign,
I will trust You in this way today...

....

....

....

You, God, say that I am...

....

....

Dear God...

....

....

....

....

....

....

....

....

....

....

....

....

....

....

How did I see God's goodness, faithfulness and sovereignty today?

....

....

Date _____ / _____ / 20_____

But you, LORD, are a shield around me, my glory,
and the one who lifts up my head.

Psalm 3:3

I am grateful for...

....

....

....

Thank You LORD that You are Good, Faithful and Sovereign,
I will trust You in this way today...

....

....

....

You, God, say that I am...

....

....

Dear God...

....

....

....

....

....

....

....

....

....

....

....

....

....

....

How did I see God's goodness, faithfulness and sovereignty today?

....

....

Date _____ / _____ / 20_____

The LORD will fight for you, and you must be quiet.

I am grateful for...

....
....
....

Thank You LORD that You are Good, Faithful and Sovereign,
I will trust You in this way today...

....
....
....

You, God, say that I am...

....
....

Dear God...

....
....
....
....
....
....
....
....
....
....
....
....
....
....

How did I see God's goodness, faithfulness and sovereignty today?

....
....

Date _____ / _____ / 20_____

A horse is prepared for the day of battle,
but victory comes from the Lord.

Proverbs 21:31

I am grateful for...

....

....

....

Thank You LORD that You are Good, Faithful and Sovereign,
I will trust You in this way today...

....

....

....

You, God, say that I am...

....

....

Dear God...

....

....

....

....

....

....

....

....

....

....

....

....

....

....

How did I see God's goodness, faithfulness and sovereignty today?

....

....

Date _____ / _____ / 20_____

I will boast in the LORD; the humble will hear and be glad.

Psalm 34:2

I am grateful for...

....

....

....

Thank You LORD that You are Good, Faithful and Sovereign,
I will trust You in this way today...

....

....

....

You, God, say that I am...

....

....

Dear God...

....

....

....

....

....

....

....

....

....

....

....

....

....

....

How did I see God's goodness, faithfulness and sovereignty today?

....

....

Date _____ / _____ / 20_____

I am the good shepherd. I know my own, and my own know me.

I am grateful for...

....
....
....

Thank You LORD that You are Good, Faithful and Sovereign,
I will trust You in this way today...

....
....
....

You, God, say that I am...

....
....

Dear God...

....
....
....
....
....
....
....
....
....
....
....
....
....
....

How did I see God's goodness, faithfulness and sovereignty today?

....
....

Date _____ / _____ / 20_____

*But these are written so that you may believe that Jesus
is the Messiah, the Son of God, and that by believing
you may have life in his name.*

John 20:31

I am grateful for...

....

....

....

Thank You LORD that You are Good, Faithful and Sovereign,
I will trust You in this way today...

....

....

....

You, God, say that I am...

....

....

Dear God...

....

....

....

....

....

....

....

....

....

....

....

....

....

....

....

How did I see God's goodness, faithfulness and sovereignty today?

....

....

Date _____ / _____ / 20_____

I -- I sweep away your transgressions for my own sake and remember your sins no more.

Isaiah 43:25

I am grateful for...

....

....

....

Thank You LORD that You are Good, Faithful and Sovereign,
I will trust You in this way today...

....

....

....

You, God, say that I am...

....

....

Dear God...

....

....

....

....

....

....

....

....

....

....

....

....

....

....

How did I see God's goodness, faithfulness and sovereignty today?

....

....

Date _____ / _____ / 20_____

I will bless the LORD at all times; his praise will always be on my lips.

Psalm 34:1

I am grateful for...

....

....

....

Thank You LORD that You are Good, Faithful and Sovereign,
I will trust You in this way today...

....

....

....

You, God, say that I am...

....

....

Dear God...

....

....

....

....

....

....

....

....

....

....

....

....

....

....

How did I see God's goodness, faithfulness and sovereignty today?

....

....

Date _____ / _____ / 20_____

And I will be a Father to you, and you will be sons and daughters to me, says the Lord Almighty.

2 Corinthians 6:18

I am grateful for...

....

....

....

Thank You LORD that You are Good, Faithful and Sovereign,
I will trust You in this way today...

....

....

....

You, God, say that I am...

....

....

Dear God...

....

....

....

....

....

....

....

....

....

....

....

....

....

....

How did I see God's goodness, faithfulness and sovereignty today?

....

....

Date _____ / _____ / 20_____

They conquered him by the blood of the Lamb and by the word of their testimony; for they did not love their lives to the point of death.

Revelation 12:11

I am grateful for...

....

....

....

Thank You LORD that You are Good, Faithful and Sovereign,
I will trust You in this way today...

....

....

....

You, God, say that I am...

....

....

Dear God...

....

....

....

....

....

....

....

....

....

....

....

....

....

....

How did I see God's goodness, faithfulness and sovereignty today?

....

....

Date _____ / _____ / 20_____

The LORD is my strength and my shield; my heart trusts in him,
and I am helped. Therefore my heart celebrates,
and I give thanks to him with my song.

Psalm 28:7

I am grateful for...

....

....

....

Thank You LORD that You are Good, Faithful and Sovereign,
I will trust You in this way today...

....

....

....

You, God, say that I am...

....

....

Dear God...

....

....

....

....

....

....

....

....

....

....

....

....

....

....

How did I see God's goodness, faithfulness and sovereignty today?

....

....

Date _____ / _____ / 20____

So faith comes from what is heard, and what is heard comes through the message about Christ.

Romans 10:17

I am grateful for...

....

....

....

Thank You LORD that You are Good, Faithful and Sovereign,
I will trust You in this way today...

....

....

....

You, God, say that I am...

....

....

Dear God...

....

....

....

....

....

....

....

....

....

....

....

....

....

How did I see God's goodness, faithfulness and sovereignty today?

....

....

Date _____ / _____ / 20_____

In him was life, and that life was the light of men.

John 1:4

I am grateful for...

....

....

....

Thank You LORD that You are Good, Faithful and Sovereign,
I will trust You in this way today...

....

....

....

You, God, say that I am...

....

....

Dear God...

....

....

....

....

....

....

....

....

....

....

....

....

....

....

How did I see God's goodness, faithfulness and sovereignty today?

....

....

Date _____ / _____ / 20_____

In him we have redemption through his blood, the forgiveness of our trespasses, according to the riches of his grace that he richly poured out on us with all wisdom and understanding.

I am grateful for...   *Ephesians 1:7-8*

....

....

....

Thank You LORD that You are Good, Faithful and Sovereign,
I will trust You in this way today...

....

....

....

You, God, say that I am...

....

....

Dear God...

....

....

....

....

....

....

....

....

....

....

....

....

....

How did I see God's goodness, faithfulness and sovereignty today?

....

....

Date _____ / _____ / 20_____

Those who know your name trust in you because you have not abandoned those who seek you, LORD.

Psalm 9:10

I am grateful for...

....

....

....

Thank You LORD that You are Good, Faithful and Sovereign,
I will trust You in this way today...

....

....

....

You, God, say that I am...

....

....

Dear God...

....

....

....

....

....

....

....

....

....

....

....

....

....

....

How did I see God's goodness, faithfulness and sovereignty today?

....

....

Date _____ / _____ / 20_____

But I will look to the LORD; I will wait for the God of my salvation.
My God will hear me.

Micah 7:7

I am grateful for...

....

....

....

Thank You LORD that You are Good, Faithful and Sovereign,
I will trust You in this way today...

....

....

....

You, God, say that I am...

....

....

Dear God...

....

....

....

....

....

....

....

....

....

....

....

....

....

....

How did I see God's goodness, faithfulness and sovereignty today?

....

....

Date _____ / _____ / 20_____

For we do not have a high priest who is unable to sympathize with our weaknesses, but one who has been tempted in every way as we are, yet without sin.

I am grateful for...   *Hebrews 4:15*

....

....

....

Thank You LORD that You are Good, Faithful and Sovereign,
I will trust You in this way today...

....

....

....

You, God, say that I am...

....

....

Dear God...

....

....

....

....

....

....

....

....

....

....

....

....

....

....

How did I see God's goodness, faithfulness and sovereignty today?

....

....

Date _____ / _____ / 20_____

The LORD is a refuge for the persecuted, a refuge in times of trouble.

Psalm 9:9

I am grateful for...

....

....

....

Thank You LORD that You are Good, Faithful and Sovereign,
I will trust You in this way today...

....

....

....

You, God, say that I am...

....

....

Dear God...

....

....

....

....

....

....

....

....

....

....

....

....

....

How did I see God's goodness, faithfulness and sovereignty today?

....

....

Date _____ / _____ / 20_____

The fear of the LORD is the beginning of knowledge;
fools despise wisdom and discipline.

Proverbs 1:7

I am grateful for...

....

....

....

Thank You LORD that You are Good, Faithful and Sovereign,
I will trust You in this way today...

....

....

....

You, God, say that I am...

....

....

Dear God...

....

....

....

....

....

....

....

....

....

....

....

....

....

....

How did I see God's goodness, faithfulness and sovereignty today?

....

....

Date _____ / _____ / 20_____

Looking at them, Jesus said, "With man it is impossible, but not with God, because all things are possible with God."

Mark 10:27

I am grateful for...

....

....

....

Thank You LORD that You are Good, Faithful and Sovereign,
I will trust You in this way today...

....

....

....

You, God, say that I am...

....

....

Dear God...

....

....

....

....

....

....

....

....

....

....

....

....

....

....

How did I see God's goodness, faithfulness and sovereignty today?

....

....

Date _____ / _____ / 20_____

And we have come to know and to believe the love that God has for us.
God is love, and the one who remains in love remains in God,
and God remains in him.

I am grateful for...   1 John 4:16

....

....

....

Thank You LORD that You are Good, Faithful and Sovereign,
I will trust You in this way today...

....

....

....

You, God, say that I am...

....

....

Dear God...

....

....

....

....

....

....

....

....

....

....

....

....

....

How did I see God's goodness, faithfulness and sovereignty today?

....

....

Date _____ / _____ / 20____

LORD, be pleased to rescue me; hurry to help me, LORD.

Psalm 40:13

I am grateful for...

....

....

....

Thank You LORD that You are Good, Faithful and Sovereign,
I will trust You in this way today...

....

....

....

You, God, say that I am...

....

....

Dear God...

....

....

....

....

....

....

....

....

....

....

....

....

....

....

How did I see God's goodness, faithfulness and sovereignty today?

....

....

Date _____ / _____ / 20_____

Do not be conformed to this age, but be transformed by the renewing of your mind, so that you may discern what is the good, pleasing, and perfect will of God.

I am grateful for...   *Romans 12:2*

....

....

....

Thank You LORD that You are Good, Faithful and Sovereign,
I will trust You in this way today...

....

....

....

You, God, say that I am...

....

....

Dear God...

....

....

....

....

....

....

....

....

....

....

....

....

....

How did I see God's goodness, faithfulness and sovereignty today?

....

....

Date _____ / _____ / 20_____

Let us be glad, rejoice, and give him glory, because the marriage of the Lamb has come, and his bride has prepared herself.

Revelation 19:7

I am grateful for...

....

....

....

Thank You LORD that You are Good, Faithful and Sovereign,
I will trust You in this way today...

....

....

....

You, God, say that I am...

....

....

Dear God...

....

....

....

....

....

....

....

....

....

....

....

....

....

....

How did I see God's goodness, faithfulness and sovereignty today?

....

....

Date _____ / _____ / 20_____

Restore the joy of your salvation to me,
and sustain me by giving me a willing spirit.

Psalm 51:12

I am grateful for...

....

....

....

Thank You LORD that You are Good, Faithful and Sovereign,
I will trust You in this way today...

....

....

....

You, God, say that I am...

....

....

Dear God...

....

....

....

....

....

....

....

....

....

....

....

....

....

How did I see God's goodness, faithfulness and sovereignty today?

....

....

Date _____ / _____ / 20_____

I have learned to be content in whatever circumstances I find myself.
I know both how to make do with little, and I know how to make do
with a lot,...I am able to do all things through him who strengthens me.

I am grateful for...   *Phillipians 4:11b,12a,13*

....

....

....

Thank You LORD that You are Good, Faithful and Sovereign,
I will trust You in this way today...

....

....

....

You, God, say that I am...

....

....

Dear God...

....

....

....

....

....

....

....

....

....

....

....

....

....

....

How did I see God's goodness, faithfulness and sovereignty today?

....

....

Date _____ / _____ / 20_____

Do not judge, and you will not be judged. Do not condemn, and you will not be condemned. Forgive, and you will be forgiven.

I am grateful for...

....

....

....

Thank You LORD that You are Good, Faithful and Sovereign,
I will trust You in this way today...

....

....

....

You, God, say that I am...

....

....

Dear God...

....

....

....

....

....

....

....

....

....

....

....

....

....

How did I see God's goodness, faithfulness and sovereignty today?

....

....

Date _____ / _____ / 20_____

Therefore, as God's chosen ones, holy and dearly loved, put on compassion, kindness, humility, gentleness, and patience.

Colossians 3:12

I am grateful for...

....
....
....

Thank You LORD that You are Good, Faithful and Sovereign,
I will trust You in this way today...

....
....
....

You, God, say that I am...

....
....

Dear God...

....
....
....
....
....
....
....
....
....
....
....
....
....

How did I see God's goodness, faithfulness and sovereignty today?

....
....

Date _____ / _____ / 20_____

LORD, you do not withhold your compassion from me.
Your constant love and truth will always guard me.

Psalm 40:11

I am grateful for...

....

....

....

Thank You LORD that You are Good, Faithful and Sovereign,
I will trust You in this way today...

....

....

....

You, God, say that I am...

....

....

Dear God...

....

....

....

....

....

....

....

....

....

....

....

....

....

....

How did I see God's goodness, faithfulness and sovereignty today?

....

....

Date _____ / _____ / 20_____

Throw off all the transgressions you have committed,
and get yourselves a new heart and a new spirit.

I am grateful for...   *Ezekiel 18:31*

....

....

....

Thank You LORD that You are Good, Faithful and Sovereign,
I will trust You in this way today...

....

....

....

You, God, say that I am...

....

....

Dear God...

....

....

....

....

....

....

....

....

....

....

....

....

....

How did I see God's goodness, faithfulness and sovereignty today?

....

....

Date _____ / _____ / 20_____

I am the good shepherd.
The good shepherd lays down his life for the sheep.

John 10:11

I am grateful for...

....

....

....

Thank You LORD that You are Good, Faithful and Sovereign,
I will trust You in this way today...

....

....

....

You, God, say that I am...

....

....

Dear God...

....

....

....

....

....

....

....

....

....

....

....

....

....

....

How did I see God's goodness, faithfulness and sovereignty today?

....

....

Date _____ / _____ / 20_____

You yourself have recorded my wanderings.
Put my tears in your bottle. Are they not in your book?

Psalm 56:8

I am grateful for...

....

....

....

Thank You LORD that You are Good, Faithful and Sovereign,
I will trust You in this way today...

....

....

....

You, God, say that I am...

....

....

Dear God...

....

....

....

....

....

....

....

....

....

....

....

....

....

....

How did I see God's goodness, faithfulness and sovereignty today?

....

....

Date _____ / _____ / 20_____

Therefore, we are ambassadors for Christ, since God is making his appeal through us. We plead on Christ's behalf: Be reconciled to God.

2 Corinthians 5:20

I am grateful for...

....

....

....

Thank You LORD that You are Good, Faithful and Sovereign,
I will trust You in this way today...

....

....

....

You, God, say that I am...

....

....

Dear God...

....

....

....

....

....

....

....

....

....

....

....

....

....

....

How did I see God's goodness, faithfulness and sovereignty today?

....

....

Date _____ / _____ / 20_____

*I waited patiently for the LORD, and he turned to me
and heard my cry for help.*

Psalm 40:1

I am grateful for...

....
....
....

Thank You LORD that You are Good, Faithful and Sovereign,
I will trust You in this way today...

....
....
....

You, God, say that I am...

....
....

Dear God...

....
....
....
....
....
....
....
....
....
....
....
....
....
....

How did I see God's goodness, faithfulness and sovereignty today?

....
....

Date _____ / _____ / 20_____

Now may the God of hope fill you with all joy and peace as you believe so that you may overflow with hope by the power of the Holy Spirit.

Romans 15:13

I am grateful for...

....

....

....

Thank You LORD that You are Good, Faithful and Sovereign,
I will trust You in this way today...

....

....

....

You, God, say that I am...

....

....

Dear God...

....

....

....

....

....

....

....

....

....

....

....

....

....

....

How did I see God's goodness, faithfulness and sovereignty today?

....

....

Date _____ / _____ / 20_____

I am the vine; you are the branches. The one who remains in me and I in him produces much fruit, because you can do nothing without me.

John 15:5

I am grateful for...

....

....

....

Thank You LORD that You are Good, Faithful and Sovereign, I will trust You in this way today...

....

....

....

You, God, say that I am...

....

....

Dear God...

....

....

....

....

....

....

....

....

....

....

....

....

....

....

How did I see God's goodness, faithfulness and sovereignty today?

....

....

Date _____ / _____ / 20_____

LORD my God, you have done many things -- your wondrous works and your plans for us; none can compare with you. If I were to report and speak of them, they are more than can be told.

I am grateful for...   *Psalm 40:5*

....

....

....

Thank You LORD that You are Good, Faithful and Sovereign,
I will trust You in this way today...

....

....

....

You, God, say that I am...

....

....

Dear God...

....

....

....

....

....

....

....

....

....

....

....

....

....

How did I see God's goodness, faithfulness and sovereignty today?

....

....

Date _____ / _____ / 20_____

You do not have to fight this battle. Position yourselves, stand still, and see the salvation of the LORD.

2 Chronicles 20:17a

I am grateful for...

....

....

....

Thank You LORD that You are Good, Faithful and Sovereign,
I will trust You in this way today...

....

....

....

You, God, say that I am...

....

....

Dear God...

....

....

....

....

....

....

....

....

....

....

....

....

....

How did I see God's goodness, faithfulness and sovereignty today?

....

....

Date _____ / _____ / 20_____

He brought me up from a desolate pit, out of the muddy clay, and set my feet on a rock, making my steps secure.

Psalm 40:2

I am grateful for...

....

....

....

Thank You LORD that You are Good, Faithful and Sovereign,
I will trust You in this way today...

....

....

....

You, God, say that I am...

....

....

Dear God...

....

....

....

....

....

....

....

....

....

....

....

....

....

....

How did I see God's goodness, faithfulness and sovereignty today?

....

....

Date _____ / _____ / 20_____

For this reason take up the full armor of God, so that you may be able to resist in the evil day, and having prepared everything, to take your stand.

Ephesians 6:13

I am grateful for...

....

....

....

Thank You LORD that You are Good, Faithful and Sovereign,
I will trust You in this way today...

....

....

....

You, God, say that I am...

....

....

Dear God...

....

....

....

....

....

....

....

....

....

....

....

....

....

....

How did I see God's goodness, faithfulness and sovereignty today?

....

....

Date _____ / _____ / 20_____

God will bring this about in his own time. He is the blessed and
only Sovereign, the King of kings, and the Lord of lords.

1 Timothy 6:15

I am grateful for...

....

....

....

Thank You LORD that You are Good, Faithful and Sovereign,
I will trust You in this way today...

....

....

....

You, God, say that I am...

....

....

Dear God...

....

....

....

....

....

....

....

....

....

....

....

....

....

....

How did I see God's goodness, faithfulness and sovereignty today?

....

....

Date _____ / _____ / 20_____

But you are holy, enthroned on the praises of Israel.

Psalm 22:3

I am grateful for...

....
....
....

Thank You LORD that You are Good, Faithful and Sovereign,
I will trust You in this way today...

....
....
....

You, God, say that I am...

....
....

Dear God...

....
....
....
....
....
....
....
....
....
....
....
....
....
....

How did I see God's goodness, faithfulness and sovereignty today?

....
....

Date _____ / _____ / 20_____

He brought me to the banquet hall, and he looked on me with love.

Song of Songs 2:4

I am grateful for...

....
....
....

Thank You LORD that You are Good, Faithful and Sovereign,
I will trust You in this way today...

....
....
....

You, God, say that I am...

....
....

Dear God...

....
....
....
....
....
....
....
....
....
....
....
....
....
....

How did I see God's goodness, faithfulness and sovereignty today?

....
....

Date _____ / _____ / 20_____

A thief comes only to steal and kill and destroy. I have come so that they may have life and have it in abundance.

John 10:10

I am grateful for...

....

....

....

Thank You LORD that You are Good, Faithful and Sovereign,
I will trust You in this way today...

....

....

....

You, God, say that I am...

....

....

Dear God...

....

....

....

....

....

....

....

....

....

....

....

....

....

....

How did I see God's goodness, faithfulness and sovereignty today?

....

....

Date _____ / _____ / 20_____

I am certain that I will see the LORD's goodness in the land of the living. Wait for the LORD; be strong, and let your heart be courageous. Wait for the LORD.

Psalm 27:13-14

I am grateful for...

....

....

....

Thank You LORD that You are Good, Faithful and Sovereign,
I will trust You in this way today...

....

....

....

You, God, say that I am...

....

....

Dear God...

....

....

....

....

....

....

....

....

....

....

....

....

....

....

How did I see God's goodness, faithfulness and sovereignty today?

....

....

Date _____ / _____ / 20_____

Love is patient, love is kind. Love does not envy, is not boastful, is not arrogant,... Love finds no joy in unrighteousness but rejoices in the truth. It bears all things, believes all things, hopes all things, endures all things.

I am grateful for...

....

....

....

Thank You LORD that You are Good, Faithful and Sovereign,
I will trust You in this way today...

....

....

....

You, God, say that I am...

....

....

Dear God...

....

....

....

....

....

....

....

....

....

....

....

....

....

....

How did I see God's goodness, faithfulness and sovereignty today?

....

....

Date _____ / _____ / 20_____

Therefore, there is now no condemnation for those in Christ Jesus.

Romans 8:1

I am grateful for...

....

....

....

Thank You LORD that You are Good, Faithful and Sovereign,
I will trust You in this way today...

....

....

....

You, God, say that I am...

....

....

Dear God...

....

....

....

....

....

....

....

....

....

....

....

....

....

....

How did I see God's goodness, faithfulness and sovereignty today?

....

....

Date _____ / _____ / 20_____

Before a word is on my tongue, you know all about it, LORD. You have encircled me; you have placed your hand on me. This wondrous knowledge is beyond me. It is lofty; I am unable to reach it.

I am grateful for...   *Psalm 139:4-6*

....
....
....

Thank You LORD that You are Good, Faithful and Sovereign,
I will trust You in this way today...

....
....
....

You, God, say that I am...

....
....

Dear God...

....
....
....
....
....
....
....
....
....
....
....
....
....

How did I see God's goodness, faithfulness and sovereignty today?

....
....

Date _____ / _____ / 20_____

So he got up and went to his father. But while the son was still a long way off, his father saw him and was filled with compassion. He ran, threw his arms around his neck, and kissed him.

Luke 15:20

I am grateful for...

....

....

....

Thank You LORD that You are Good, Faithful and Sovereign,
I will trust You in this way today...

....

....

....

You, God, say that I am...

....

....

Dear God...

....

....

....

....

....

....

....

....

....

....

....

....

....

....

How did I see God's goodness, faithfulness and sovereignty today?

....

....

Date _____ / _____ / 20_____

In him we have redemption, the forgiveness of sins.

Colossians 1:14

I am grateful for...

....

....

....

Thank You LORD that You are Good, Faithful and Sovereign,
I will trust You in this way today...

....

....

....

You, God, say that I am...

....

....

Dear God...

....

....

....

....

....

....

....

....

....

....

....

....

....

....

How did I see God's goodness, faithfulness and sovereignty today?

....

....

Date _____ / _____ / 20_____

My steps are on your paths; my feet have not slipped.

Psalm 17:5

I am grateful for...

....

....

....

Thank You LORD that You are Good, Faithful and Sovereign,
I will trust You in this way today...

....

....

....

You, God, say that I am...

....

....

Dear God...

....

....

....

....

....

....

....

....

....

....

....

....

....

....

How did I see God's goodness, faithfulness and sovereignty today?

....

....

Date _____ / _____ / 20_____

I will praise you because I have been remarkably and wondrously made. Your works are wondrous, and I know this very well.

Psalm 139:14

I am grateful for...

....

....

....

Thank You LORD that You are Good, Faithful and Sovereign,
I will trust You in this way today...

....

....

....

You, God, say that I am...

....

....

Dear God...

....

....

....

....

....

....

....

....

....

....

....

....

....

....

How did I see God's goodness, faithfulness and sovereignty today?

....

....

Date _____ / _____ / 20_____

But David found strength in the LORD his God.

1 Samuel 30:6b

I am grateful for...

....

....

....

Thank You LORD that You are Good, Faithful and Sovereign,
I will trust You in this way today...

....

....

....

You, God, say that I am...

....

....

Dear God...

....

....

....

....

....

....

....

....

....

....

....

....

....

....

How did I see God's goodness, faithfulness and sovereignty today?

....

....

Date _____ / _____ / 20_____

Love the Lord your God with all your heart, with all your soul,
with all your mind, and with all your strength.

Mark 12:30

I am grateful for...

....

....

....

Thank You LORD that You are Good, Faithful and Sovereign,
I will trust You in this way today...

....

....

....

You, God, say that I am...

....

....

Dear God...

....

....

....

....

....

....

....

....

....

....

....

....

....

....

How did I see God's goodness, faithfulness and sovereignty today?

....

....

Date _____ / _____ / 20_____

Come to me, all of you who are weary and burdened,
and I will give you rest.

Matthew 11:28

I am grateful for...

....

....

....

Thank You LORD that You are Good, Faithful and Sovereign,
I will trust You in this way today...

....

....

....

You, God, say that I am...

....

....

Dear God...

....

....

....

....

....

....

....

....

....

....

....

....

....

....

How did I see God's goodness, faithfulness and sovereignty today?

....

....

Date _____ / _____ / 20_____

Even when I go through the darkest valley, I fear no danger,
for you are with me; your rod and your staff - they comfort me.

Psalm 23:4

I am grateful for...

....

....

....

Thank You LORD that You are Good, Faithful and Sovereign,
I will trust You in this way today...

....

....

....

You, God, say that I am...

....

....

Dear God...

....

....

....

....

....

....

....

....

....

....

....

....

....

....

How did I see God's goodness, faithfulness and sovereignty today?

....

....

Date _____ / _____ / 20_____

No temptation has come upon you except what is common to humanity.
But God is faithful; he will not allow you to be tempted beyond
what you are able, but with the temptation he will also provide a way out
so that you may be able to bear it.
I am grateful for...   *1 Corinthians 10:13*

....

....

....

Thank You LORD that You are Good, Faithful and Sovereign,
I will trust You in this way today...

....

....

....

You, God, say that I am...

....

....

Dear God...

....

....

....

....

....

....

....

....

....

....

....

....

....

....

How did I see God's goodness, faithfulness and sovereignty today?

....

....

Date _____ / _____ / 20_____

The person who trusts in the LORD... is blessed. He will be like a tree
planted by water: it sends its roots out toward a stream, it doesn't fear
when heat comes, and its foliage remains green. It will not worry in a year
of drought or cease producing fruit.

I am grateful for...   *Jeremiah 17:7-8*

....

....

....

Thank You LORD that You are Good, Faithful and Sovereign,
I will trust You in this way today...

....

....

....

You, God, say that I am...

....

....

Dear God...

....

....

....

....

....

....

....

....

....

....

....

....

....

....

How did I see God's goodness, faithfulness and sovereignty today?

....

....

Date _____ / _____ / 20____

The LORD is my light and my salvation -- whom should I fear?
The LORD is the stronghold of my life -- whom should I dread?

Psalm 27:1

I am grateful for...

....

....

....

Thank You LORD that You are Good, Faithful and Sovereign,
I will trust You in this way today...

....

....

....

You, God, say that I am...

....

....

Dear God...

....

....

....

....

....

....

....

....

....

....

....

....

....

....

How did I see God's goodness, faithfulness and sovereignty today?

....

....

Date _____ / _____ / 20_____

But you are a chosen race, a royal priesthood, a holy nation, a people for his possession, so that you may proclaim the praises of the one who called you out of darkness into his marvelous light.

1 Peter 2:9

I am grateful for...

....

....

....

Thank You LORD that You are Good, Faithful and Sovereign,
I will trust You in this way today...

....

....

....

You, God, say that I am...

....

....

Dear God...

....

....

....

....

....

....

....

....

....

....

....

....

How did I see God's goodness, faithfulness and sovereignty today?

....

....

Date _____ / _____ / 20_____

Thanks be to God through Jesus Christ our Lord! So then, with my mind I myself am serving the law of God, but with my flesh, the law of sin. Romans 7:25

I am grateful for...

....

....

....

Thank You LORD that You are Good, Faithful and Sovereign,
I will trust You in this way today...

....

....

....

You, God, say that I am...

....

....

Dear God...

....

....

....

....

....

....

....

....

....

....

....

....

....

....

How did I see God's goodness, faithfulness and sovereignty today?

....

....

Date _____ / _____ / 20_____

Let a wise person listen and increase learning,
and let a discerning person obtain guidance.

I am grateful for...   *Proverbs 1:5*

....
....
....

Thank You LORD that You are Good, Faithful and Sovereign,
I will trust You in this way today...

....
....
....

You, God, say that I am...

....
....

Dear God...

....
....
....
....
....
....
....
....
....
....
....
....
....

How did I see God's goodness, faithfulness and sovereignty today?

....
....

Date _____ / _____ / 20_____

Display the wonders of your faithful love, Savior of all who seek refuge from those who rebel against your right hand.

Psalm 17:7

I am grateful for...

....

....

....

Thank You LORD that You are Good, Faithful and Sovereign,
I will trust You in this way today...

....

....

....

You, God, say that I am...

....

....

Dear God...

....

....

....

....

....

....

....

....

....

....

....

....

....

....

How did I see God's goodness, faithfulness and sovereignty today?

....

....

Date _____ / _____ / 20_____

My Father is glorified by this: that you produce much fruit and prove to be my disciples.

I am grateful for...

....

....

....

Thank You LORD that You are Good, Faithful and Sovereign,
I will trust You in this way today...

....

....

....

You, God, say that I am...

....

....

Dear God...

....

....

....

....

....

....

....

....

....

....

....

....

....

....

How did I see God's goodness, faithfulness and sovereignty today?

....

....

Date _____ / _____ / 20_____

Therefore, let us approach the throne of grace with boldness, so that we may receive mercy and find grace to help us in time of need.

Hebrews 4:16

I am grateful for...

....
....
....

Thank You LORD that You are Good, Faithful and Sovereign,
I will trust You in this way today...

....
....
....

You, God, say that I am...

....
....

Dear God...

....
....
....
....
....
....
....
....
....
....
....
....
....
....

How did I see God's goodness, faithfulness and sovereignty today?

....
....

Date _____ / _____ / 20_____

Rejoice in the Lord always. I will say it again: Rejoice!

Philippians 4:4

I am grateful for...

....
....
....

Thank You LORD that You are Good, Faithful and Sovereign,
I will trust You in this way today...

....
....
....

You, God, say that I am...

....
....

Dear God...

....
....
....
....
....
....
....
....
....
....
....
....
....
....

How did I see God's goodness, faithfulness and sovereignty today?

....
....

Date _____ / _____ / 20_____

My soul, bless the LORD, and do not forget all his benefits.
He forgives all your iniquity; he heals all your diseases.

Psalm 103:2-3

I am grateful for...

....

....

....

Thank You LORD that You are Good, Faithful and Sovereign,
I will trust You in this way today...

....

....

....

You, God, say that I am...

....

....

Dear God...

....

....

....

....

....

....

....

....

....

....

....

....

....

....

How did I see God's goodness, faithfulness and sovereignty today?

....

....

Date _____ / _____ / 20_____

No weapon formed against you will succeed.

Isaiah 54:17a

I am grateful for...

....

....

....

Thank You LORD that You are Good, Faithful and Sovereign,
I will trust You in this way today...

....

....

....

You, God, say that I am...

....

....

Dear God...

....

....

....

....

....

....

....

....

....

....

....

....

....

....

How did I see God's goodness, faithfulness and sovereignty today?

....

....

Date _____ / _____ / 20_____

If the world hates you, understand that it hated me
before it hated you.

John 15:18

I am grateful for...

....

....

....

Thank You LORD that You are Good, Faithful and Sovereign,
I will trust You in this way today...

....

....

....

You, God, say that I am...

....

....

Dear God...

....

....

....

....

....

....

....

....

....

....

....

....

....

How did I see God's goodness, faithfulness and sovereignty today?

....

....

Date _____ / _____ / 20_____

Cast your burden on the LORD, and he will sustain you;
he will never allow the righteous to be shaken.

Psalm 55:22

I am grateful for...

....

....

....

Thank You LORD that You are Good, Faithful and Sovereign,
I will trust You in this way today...

....

....

....

You, God, say that I am...

....

....

Dear God...

....

....

....

....

....

....

....

....

....

....

....

....

....

....

How did I see God's goodness, faithfulness and sovereignty today?

....

....

Date _____ / _____ / 20_____

He also raised us up with him and seated us with him in the heavens in Christ Jesus.

Ephesians 2:6

I am grateful for...

....

....

....

Thank You LORD that You are Good, Faithful and Sovereign,
I will trust You in this way today...

....

....

....

You, God, say that I am...

....

....

Dear God...

....

....

....

....

....

....

....

....

....

....

....

....

....

....

How did I see God's goodness, faithfulness and sovereignty today?

....

....

Date _____ / _____ / 20_____

We know that all things work together for the good of those who love God, who are called according to his purpose.

Romans 8:28

I am grateful for...

....
....
....

Thank You LORD that You are Good, Faithful and Sovereign,
I will trust You in this way today...

....
....
....

You, God, say that I am...

....
....

Dear God...

....
....
....
....
....
....
....
....
....
....
....
....
....
....

How did I see God's goodness, faithfulness and sovereignty today?

....
....

Date _____ / _____ / 20_____

Being strengthened with all power, according to his glorious might,
so that you may have great endurance and patience, joyfully.

I am grateful for...

....
....
....

Thank You LORD that You are Good, Faithful and Sovereign,
I will trust You in this way today...

....
....
....

You, God, say that I am...

....
....

Dear God...

....
....
....
....
....
....
....
....
....
....
....
....
....
....

How did I see God's goodness, faithfulness and sovereignty today?

....
....

Date _____ / _____ / 20_____

May integrity and what is right watch over me, for I wait for you.

Psalm 25:21

I am grateful for...

....

....

....

Thank You LORD that You are Good, Faithful and Sovereign,
I will trust You in this way today...

....

....

....

You, God, say that I am...

....

....

Dear God...

....

....

....

....

....

....

....

....

....

....

....

....

....

....

How did I see God's goodness, faithfulness and sovereignty today?

....

....

Date _____ / _____ / 20_____

And God is able to make every grace overflow to you,
so that in every way, always having everything you need,
you may excel in every good work.

2 Corinthians 9:8

I am grateful for...

....

....

....

Thank You LORD that You are Good, Faithful and Sovereign,
I will trust You in this way today...

....

....

....

You, God, say that I am...

....

....

Dear God...

....

....

....

....

....

....

....

....

....

....

....

....

....

How did I see God's goodness, faithfulness and sovereignty today?

....

....

Date _____ / _____ / 20_____

Then Jesus told him, "Go away, Satan! For it is written: Worship the Lord your God, and serve only him."

Matthew 4:10

I am grateful for...

....

....

....

Thank You LORD that You are Good, Faithful and Sovereign,
I will trust You in this way today...

....

....

....

You, God, say that I am...

....

....

Dear God...

....

....

....

....

....

....

....

....

....

....

....

....

....

....

How did I see God's goodness, faithfulness and sovereignty today?

....

....

Date _____ / _____ / 20_____

The LORD is my rock, my fortress, and my deliverer,
my God, my rock where I seek refuge, my shield
and the horn of my salvation, my stronghold.

Psalm 18:2

I am grateful for...

....

....

....

Thank You LORD that You are Good, Faithful and Sovereign,
I will trust You in this way today...

....

....

....

You, God, say that I am...

....

....

Dear God...

....

....

....

....

....

....

....

....

....

....

....

....

....

....

How did I see God's goodness, faithfulness and sovereignty today?

....

....

Date _____ / _____ / 20_____

If we walk in the light as he himself is in the light, we have fellowship with one another, and the blood of Jesus his Son cleanses us from all sin.

1 John 1:7

I am grateful for...

....

....

....

Thank You LORD that You are Good, Faithful and Sovereign,
I will trust You in this way today...

....

....

....

You, God, say that I am...

....

....

Dear God...

....

....

....

....

....

....

....

....

....

....

....

....

....

How did I see God's goodness, faithfulness and sovereignty today?

....

....

Date _____ / _____ / 20_____

I give you a new command: Love one another. Just as I have loved you, you are also to love one another. By this everyone will know that you are my disciples, if you love one another.

I am grateful for...   *John 13:34-35*

....

....

....

Thank You LORD that You are Good, Faithful and Sovereign,
I will trust You in this way today...

....

....

....

You, God, say that I am...

....

....

Dear God...

....

....

....

....

....

....

....

....

....

....

....

....

....

....

How did I see God's goodness, faithfulness and sovereignty today?

....

....

Date _____ / _____ / 20_____

The LORD redeems the life of his servants, and all who take refuge in him will not be punished.

Psalm 34:22

I am grateful for...

....

....

....

Thank You LORD that You are Good, Faithful and Sovereign,
I will trust You in this way today...

....

....

....

You, God, say that I am...

....

....

Dear God...

....

....

....

....

....

....

....

....

....

....

....

....

....

....

How did I see God's goodness, faithfulness and sovereignty today?

....

....

Date _____ / _____ / 20_____

He will wipe away every tear from their eyes. Death will be no more; grief, crying, and pain will be no more, because the previous things have passed away.

Revelation 21:4

I am grateful for...

....

....

....

Thank You LORD that You are Good, Faithful and Sovereign,
I will trust You in this way today...

....

....

....

You, God, say that I am...

....

....

Dear God...

....

....

....

....

....

....

....

....

....

....

....

....

....

....

How did I see God's goodness, faithfulness and sovereignty today?

....

....

Date _____ / _____ / 20_____

And my God will supply all your needs
according to his riches in glory in Christ Jesus.

Philippians 4:19

I am grateful for...

....
....
....

Thank You LORD that You are Good, Faithful and Sovereign,
I will trust You in this way today...

....
....
....

You, God, say that I am...

....
....

Dear God...

....
....
....
....
....
....
....
....
....
....
....
....
....
....

How did I see God's goodness, faithfulness and sovereignty today?

....
....

Date _____ / _____ / 20_____

Enter his gates with thanksgiving and his courts with praise.
Give thanks to him and bless his name.

I am grateful for...

....

....

....

Thank You LORD that You are Good, Faithful and Sovereign,
I will trust You in this way today...

....

....

....

You, God, say that I am...

....

....

Dear God...

....

....

....

....

....

....

....

....

....

....

....

....

....

....

How did I see God's goodness, faithfulness and sovereignty today?

....

....

Date _____ / _____ / 20_____

I am sure of this, that he who started a good work in you will carry it on to completion until the day of Christ Jesus.

Philippians 1:6

I am grateful for...

....

....

....

Thank You LORD that You are Good, Faithful and Sovereign,
I will trust You in this way today...

....

....

....

You, God, say that I am...

....

....

Dear God...

....

....

....

....

....

....

....

....

....

....

....

....

....

....

How did I see God's goodness, faithfulness and sovereignty today?

....

....

Date _____ / _____ / 20_____

And let us watch out for one another to provoke love and good works.

Hebrews 10:24

I am grateful for...

....

....

....

Thank You LORD that You are Good, Faithful and Sovereign,
I will trust You in this way today...

....

....

....

You, God, say that I am...

....

....

Dear God...

....

....

....

....

....

....

....

....

....

....

....

....

....

....

How did I see God's goodness, faithfulness and sovereignty today?

....

....

Date _____ / _____ / 20_____

But look, the LORD keeps his eye on those who fear him --
those who depend on his faithful love to rescue them from death
and to keep them alive in famine.

Psalm 33:18-19

I am grateful for...

....

....

....

Thank You LORD that You are Good, Faithful and Sovereign,
I will trust You in this way today...

....

....

....

You, God, say that I am...

....

....

Dear God...

....

....

....

....

....

....

....

....

....

....

....

....

....

....

How did I see God's goodness, faithfulness and sovereignty today?

....

....

Date _____ / _____ / 20_____

Therefore we do not give up. Even though our outer person is being destroyed, our inner person is being renewed day by day.

I am grateful for...

....

....

....

Thank You LORD that You are Good, Faithful and Sovereign,
I will trust You in this way today...

....

....

....

You, God, say that I am...

....

....

Dear God...

....

....

....

....

....

....

....

....

....

....

....

....

....

....

How did I see God's goodness, faithfulness and sovereignty today?

....

....

Date _____ / _____ / 20_____

"For I know the plans I have for you" -- this is the LORD's
declaration -- "plans for your well-being, not for disaster,
to give you a future and a hope."

Jeremiah 29:11

I am grateful for...

....

....

....

Thank You LORD that You are Good, Faithful and Sovereign,
I will trust You in this way today...

....

....

....

You, God, say that I am...

....

....

Dear God...

....

....

....

....

....

....

....

....

....

....

....

....

....

....

How did I see God's goodness, faithfulness and sovereignty today?

....

....

Date _____ / _____ / 20_____

Let all who seek you rejoice and be glad in you; let those who love your salvation continually say, "The LORD is great!"

I am grateful for...

....

....

....

Thank You LORD that You are Good, Faithful and Sovereign,
I will trust You in this way today...

....

....

....

You, God, say that I am...

....

....

Dear God...

....

....

....

....

....

....

....

....

....

....

....

....

....

How did I see God's goodness, faithfulness and sovereignty today?

....

....

Date _____ / _____ / 20_____

Search me, God, and know my heart; test me and know my concerns.
See if there is any offensive way in me; lead me in the everlasting way.

Psalm 139:23-24

I am grateful for...

....

....

....

Thank You LORD that You are Good, Faithful and Sovereign,
I will trust You in this way today...

....

....

....

You, God, say that I am...

....

....

Dear God...

....

....

....

....

....

....

....

....

....

....

....

....

....

....

How did I see God's goodness, faithfulness and sovereignty today?

....

....

Date _____ / _____ / 20_____

Therefore, since we have been declared righteous by faith,
we have peace with God through our Lord Jesus Christ.

Romans 5:1

I am grateful for...

....

....

....

Thank You LORD that You are Good, Faithful and Sovereign,
I will trust You in this way today...

....

....

....

You, God, say that I am...

....

....

Dear God...

....

....

....

....

....

....

....

....

....

....

....

....

....

....

....

How did I see God's goodness, faithfulness and sovereignty today?

....

....

Date _____ / _____ / 20_____

"Because of your little faith," he told them. *"For truly I tell you,*
if you have faith the size of a mustard seed, you will tell this mountain,
'Move from here to there,' and it will move.
Nothing will be impossible for you."

Matthew 17:20

I am grateful for...

....

....

....

Thank You LORD that You are Good, Faithful and Sovereign,
I will trust You in this way today...

....

....

....

You, God, say that I am...

....

....

Dear God...

....

....

....

....

....

....

....

....

....

....

....

....

....

....

How did I see God's goodness, faithfulness and sovereignty today?

....

....

Date _____ / _____ / 20_____

I have been crucified with Christ, and I no longer live, but Christ lives in me. The life I now live in the body, I live by faith in the Son of God, who loved me and gave himself for me.

Galations 2:20

I am grateful for...

....

....

....

Thank You LORD that You are Good, Faithful and Sovereign,
I will trust You in this way today...

....

....

....

You, God, say that I am...

....

....

Dear God...

....

....

....

....

....

....

....

....

....

....

....

....

....

....

How did I see God's goodness, faithfulness and sovereignty today?

....

....

Date _____ / _____ / 20_____

LORD, your faithful love reaches to heaven, your faithfulness to the clouds. Your righteousness is like the highest mountains, your judgments like the deepest sea. LORD, you preserve people and animals.

Psalm 36:5-6

I am grateful for...

....

....

....

Thank You LORD that You are Good, Faithful and Sovereign,
I will trust You in this way today...

....

....

....

You, God, say that I am...

....

....

Dear God...

....

....

....

....

....

....

....

....

....

....

....

....

....

....

How did I see God's goodness, faithfulness and sovereignty today?

....

....

Date _____ / _____ / 20_____

Jesus told him, "I am the way, the truth, and the life.
No one comes to the Father except through me."

I am grateful for...
John 14:6

....

....

....

Thank You LORD that You are Good, Faithful and Sovereign,
I will trust You in this way today...

....

....

....

You, God, say that I am...

....

....

Dear God...

....

....

....

....

....

....

....

....

....

....

....

....

....

....

How did I see God's goodness, faithfulness and sovereignty today?

....

....

Date _____ / _____ / 20_____

I have asked one thing from the LORD; it is what I desire: to dwell in the house of the LORD all the days of my life, gazing on the beauty of the LORD and seeking him in his temple.

Psalm 27:4

I am grateful for...

....

....

....

Thank You LORD that You are Good, Faithful and Sovereign,
I will trust You in this way today...

....

....

....

You, God, say that I am...

....

....

Dear God...

....

....

....

....

....

....

....

....

....

....

....

....

....

....

How did I see God's goodness, faithfulness and sovereignty today?

....

....

Date _____ / _____ / 20_____

For our struggle is not against flesh and blood, but against the rulers, against the authorities, against the cosmic powers of this darkness, against evil, spiritual forces in the heavens.

I am grateful for...   *Ephesians 6:12*

....

....

....

Thank You LORD that You are Good, Faithful and Sovereign,
I will trust You in this way today...

....

....

....

You, God, say that I am...

....

....

Dear God...

....

....

....

....

....

....

....

....

....

....

....

....

....

How did I see God's goodness, faithfulness and sovereignty today?

....

....

Date _____ / _____ / 20_____

The LORD is my strength and my shield; my heart trusts in him, and I am helped. Therefore my heart celebrates, and I give thanks to him with my song.

I am grateful for...   *Psalm 28:7*

....

....

....

Thank You LORD that You are Good, Faithful and Sovereign,
I will trust You in this way today...

....

....

....

You, God, say that I am...

....

....

Dear God...

....

....

....

....

....

....

....

....

....

....

....

....

....

....

How did I see God's goodness, faithfulness and sovereignty today?

....

....

Date _____ / _____ / 20_____

This is my command: Love one another as I have loved you.

John 15:12

I am grateful for...

....

....

....

Thank You LORD that You are Good, Faithful and Sovereign,
I will trust You in this way today...

....

....

....

You, God, say that I am...

....

....

Dear God...

....

....

....

....

....

....

....

....

....

....

....

....

....

....

How did I see God's goodness, faithfulness and sovereignty today?

....

....

Date _____ / _____ / 20_____

Casting all your cares on him, because he cares about you.

1 Peter 5:7

I am grateful for...

....
....
....

Thank You LORD that You are Good, Faithful and Sovereign,
I will trust You in this way today...

....
....
....

You, God, say that I am...

....
....

Dear God...

....
....
....
....
....
....
....
....
....
....
....
....
....
....

How did I see God's goodness, faithfulness and sovereignty today?

....
....

Date _____ / _____ / 20_____

He put a new song in my mouth, a hymn of praise to our God.
Many will see and fear, and they will trust in the LORD.

I am grateful for...

....

....

....

Thank You LORD that You are Good, Faithful and Sovereign,
I will trust You in this way today...

....

....

....

You, God, say that I am...

....

....

Dear God...

....

....

....

....

....

....

....

....

....

....

....

....

....

....

How did I see God's goodness, faithfulness and sovereignty today?

....

....

Date _____ / _____ / 20_____

So then, just as you have received Christ Jesus as Lord,
continue to live in him.

I am grateful for...

....

....

....

Thank You LORD that You are Good, Faithful and Sovereign,
I will trust You in this way today...

....

....

....

You, God, say that I am...

....

....

Dear God...

....

....

....

....

....

....

....

....

....

....

....

....

....

....

How did I see God's goodness, faithfulness and sovereignty today?

....

....

Date _____ / _____ / 20_____

I will not leave you as orphans; I am coming to you.

John 14:18

I am grateful for...

....

....

....

Thank You LORD that You are Good, Faithful and Sovereign,
I will trust You in this way today...

....

....

....

You, God, say that I am...

....

....

Dear God...

....

....

....

....

....

....

....

....

....

....

....

....

....

....

How did I see God's goodness, faithfulness and sovereignty today?

....

....

Date _____ / _____ / 20_____

Give thanks in everything; for this is God's will for you in Christ Jesus.

1 Thessalonians 5:18

I am grateful for...

....

....

....

Thank You LORD that You are Good, Faithful and Sovereign,
I will trust You in this way today...

....

....

....

You, God, say that I am...

....

....

Dear God...

....

....

....

....

....

....

....

....

....

....

....

....

....

....

How did I see God's goodness, faithfulness and sovereignty today?

....

....

Date _____ / _____ / 20_____

You make a spacious place beneath me for my steps,
and my ankles do not give way.

Psalm 18:36

I am grateful for...

....

....

....

Thank You LORD that You are Good, Faithful and Sovereign,
I will trust You in this way today...

....

....

....

You, God, say that I am...

....

....

Dear God...

....

....

....

....

....

....

....

....

....

....

....

....

....

....

How did I see God's goodness, faithfulness and sovereignty today?

....

....

Date _____ / _____ / 20_____

The Word became flesh and dwelt among us. We observed his glory, the glory as the one and only Son from the Father, full of grace and truth.

John 1:14

I am grateful for...

....
....
....

Thank You LORD that You are Good, Faithful and Sovereign,
I will trust You in this way today...

....
....
....

You, God, say that I am...

....
....

Dear God...

....
....
....
....
....
....
....
....
....
....
....
....
....
....

How did I see God's goodness, faithfulness and sovereignty today?

....
....

Date _____ / _____ / 20____

His master said to him, "Well done, good and faithful servant!
You were faithful over a few things; I will put you in charge of many
things. Share your master's joy."

I am grateful for...   *Matthew 25:21*

....

....

....

Thank You LORD that You are Good, Faithful and Sovereign,
I will trust You in this way today...

....

....

....

You, God, say that I am...

....

....

Dear God...

....

....

....

....

....

....

....

....

....

....

....

....

....

How did I see God's goodness, faithfulness and sovereignty today?

....

....

Date _____ / _____ / 20____

May the God of peace be with all of you. Amen.

I am grateful for...   *Romans 15:33*

....

....

....

Thank You LORD that You are Good, Faithful and Sovereign,
I will trust You in this way today...

....

....

....

You, God, say that I am...

....

....

Dear God...

....

....

....

....

....

....

....

....

....

....

....

....

....

How did I see God's goodness, faithfulness and sovereignty today?

....

....

Date _____ / _____ / 20_____

Congratulations! You've completed 180 days of your
Grateful Faith Journal. I hope you've been blessed with increasing gratefulness and faith in God. If you haven't yet, I encourage you to take a few moments to reflect on your journey.

Grateful Faith in my life ...

....

....

....

....

....

....

....

....

....

....

....

....

....

....

....

....

....

....

....

....

....

....

....

....

Acknowledgements

I would like to thank YOU for your love of God and desire to grow in your walk with Him. As with any project there are multiple people that help make it happen. I want to start with giving thanks to my friends Tracy and Justine who work at my church where I volunteer in the office. They were both so helpful and encouraging, reading through all 180 verses with keen eyes and great input. Thank you also to my new friend Katie whom I had only met in passing a few months before I knew that God had planned for her to create the beautiful cover you see. And last but definitely not least, my Husband Lars. The first one to hear about this journal, before it was a 'beyond me' project. He was supportive from the very beginning and grew even more supportive and encouraging as it came to life. Even with the verses clipped out and under our coffee table glass so I could see them, move them around, get rid of and add until I had all 180. Funny how they all fit. Hmmm, I guess God had something to do with that too! :-)

And obviously I thank God. For so much. This journal is a culmination and a beginning; proof of trust in God and what He can do and wants to do if we trust and take a step.

Do remember that He said,
>*"I will never leave you or abandon you."*
>   *Hebrews 13:5*

About the Author

Bonnie Edson is married to her sweetheart and best friend, Lars. They live in South Florida with their two dogs and enjoy staying warm all year round. Bonnie enjoys leading and participating in Bible studies and loves growing her relationship with her Creator, God.

Her favorite verse, *"But seek first the kingdom of God and his righteousness, and all these things will be provided for you." Matthew 6:33*, has been a light for her. Not everyday is it accomplished but the goal and desire has guided her through the years.

CPSIA information can be obtained
at www.ICGtesting.com
Printed in the USA
BVHW070326091019
560564BV00004B/10/P